SECOND
MESSENGERS

Wesleyan New Poets

Robert McNamara

SECOND
MESSENGERS

Wesleyan University Press
Middletown, Connecticut

I would like to acknowledge the following magazines, in which some of these poems originally appeared: *The Agni Review, The Colorado Review, Kansas Quarterly, Massachusetts Review, The Missouri Review, Poetry Northwest, The Ohio Review,* and *The Seattle Review.* "In the Hearts of His Countrymen" and "Such Accomplishments" appeared originally in *Quarterly West.*

I would also like to thank the National Endowment for the Arts for a Creative Writing Fellowship, which gave me some time (and a little leisure) to write this book.

All inquiries and permissions requests should be addressed to the Publisher, Wesleyan University Press, 110 Mt. Vernon Street, Middletown, Connecticut 06457.

LIBRARY OF CONGRESS CATALOGING-IN-PUBLICATION DATA
McNamara, Robert James.
Second messengers / Robert McNamara. — 1st ed.
    p.   cm. — (Wesleyan new poets)
Some of the poems appeared previously in Agni review, and others.
ISBN 0-8195-2182-5   ISBN 0-8195-1184-6 (pbk.)
I. Title.   II. Series.
PS3563.C38834W46   1990
811'.54 — dc20   89-32935
                                                                          CIP

Manufactured in the United States of America

FIRST EDITION

Wesleyan New Poets

for Judy

Contents

The Wound

In this blue prolific light you squint
to see a child sitting by the stream, his shirt splayed
beside him in the grass. A bamboo pole catches the brown curve
of his shoulder and the green-laden tree.

This isolation pains you:
it is a pleasant afternoon.

And this dove, like the soul sprung from the mouth
at the moment of death, as it had passed mouth to mouth
in columbine kiss . . .

His right foot moves, and you feel the cool ripple over your instep,
the wake under your arch.
The dove's eyes are yellow and shrewd.

You think the blackberries have never been so sweet!

Then it explodes, a little bluegill beating the air
like a wind-up toy, and the boy ripping the hook
from the gristly tissues of its mouth.

He listens, and you think of some saint
listening, in which painting you no longer remember, a dove
hovering at his ear as he sits at his writing table:
    Gaude, Virgo, Mater Christi,
    Quae per aurem concepisti.

For years after they covered the chemical fill with dirt
the ground would burn sometimes at night, a leapfrog
of lambent bluish flame. Coming through the cut
the boats would gather on the water, luffing their sails

in the twilight winds, the flutter and snap
lending the bickering flames a fierceness, a blue mystery
that held them, gazing, amazed.

His pole leans against the alder behind him, the hook
grazing his shoulder like a deer fly.

You begin to walk toward him, a killdeer running before you,
its wing splayed as though broken, and a dove

wiping its bill on a branch.

Three Animal Stories

One is how I wake up hard in the night
smelling you near. Another

is that my daughter wants her father
with a new woman, her mother with a new man.

A refugee's craft, this small Hmong tapestry
you have sewn into a pillow for her circles water

with ibis and deer, water buffalo, a forest-
green elephant and rhino, and birds

in colors even birds have never worn.
The third story has to do with this: the animals

drinking, the monkeys in the trees eating
the plentiful fruit, and the widening circles of water

around the ibis' leg. A bright, peaceable kingdom!
And still, as though the story was told, an after-

image, lingering. This morning I woke terrified
that you had died. On the other side, the pillow

is blank, sky blue, an ocean away, far from home.
The perfume you have added to this peasant craft

is sweet and clean. Maybe the refugee named it
"Three Animal Stories" because that's all here,

the wanting it, the gift
given and received.

Absences

Once upon a time there is a child, the child says,
who lives with his mother in a small house in the city.
One day a monster comes and eats the child. The mother
cries and cries until she disappears. In the belly
of the monster, who is smiling, the child smiles too.

Something has taken my breath away and again
I am somewhere else, out
ahead of myself, behind in my work, lost
in thought. It is an unseasonable afternoon,

and I am at the fence, resting my chin on my arm:

horses graze, shimmering in the heat, at the shadowed edges
of the field. Men are lying in each other's arms.
Or the water, the glittering and shallow double
of the white shaft erected *pro patri*, mother country,

and then in phalanx, nightsticks like stripped antennae,
a carapace of bright shields . . .

I forgot, you say, as though this leaving out were not
the tissue of your life, and watch them work

as though in some other young boy's eyes they pour this
sterile wash of sucrose and salts to flush the lye.
You joke, above it all, your mother waiting, weeping, and you
taking care of her in this hour of need
because her absence is more painful even than this.

Silent in the cat's favorite armchair, you smile at what you know
should give you pleasure and will not. You have nothing

but the too-insistent fruits of your intellect, a little
too serious for the present circumstances
(party and dance).

(Your father's wounds were superficial but ugly.
He sat there like an injured child, saying nothing,

or that everything, everything just seemed so important
this week, things at work and at home, and I just wanted
to let you know that, and that
I'm really looking forward to what comes next for us, because that
will be special too, a real challenge, and exciting

in its own way, smooth as ice.)

Certain Pleasures

Sometimes having everything right would mean
you, and those certain pleasures sometimes, might mean
no end of the longing strings, the old song

with a dozen names like "I've Got a Crush on You" or
"Guess I'll Hang My Tears Out to Dry." Here's the picture:

a field of sere and wind-rippled autumn grass that rises
toward a not-too-distant farmhouse, or the light cascading
from an opening sky, mountains' majesty. As my hands inch

to reach for you, they grow cold, afraid, and I am adrift
in an old sadness. So with these beautiful still
lifes, these meticulous floral arrangements,

and the injuries on which their beauty depends.
And over there, see how that lemon is changed where
it is the only fruit beside the heap of cleaned fish.

Why I Cannot Begin, Dear Friend

Perhaps I heard nothing all those years, saw you for myself,
her friend and mine, joining us in food and close talk,
or those brilliant summer afternoons. Perhaps

I knew you were making love to her the way one knows that
the man on the bench is waiting for no one, though
he looks at his watch, taps his foot, folds and unfolds

his paper. I've wanted to kill you, and some days the sound
of people I love talking in the next room, talking in the cautious
tones of the half-empty elevator, leaning so that the breath

and flicker of the lips arouse the listener's ear,
is enough. You say that you loved us both,
I would not trap her or another, yet who does not know

how resolutely we dress for hard weather, and the soft place
we shelter underneath? Did you think you could swallow
these contradictions? Love may be a crane or a sparrow,

this hard place, that blackness expanding, drawing us all in
and down. I wonder how you spoke to yourself
as we walked the beach, or alone in your room, looking out toward

the wavebreak, or in. What true beginning did you compose
for this doubling middle? I loved you, was touched
by your griefs then, such as you opened,

joyed as I could in what happinesss you allowed yourself
to feel or say. Asking what was there: this wound is deepest,
was least expected, will be last to heal. Do not imagine

this will change, or wait on this sky, these clouds hanging an unflattering backdrop for the trees. I can't forgive you this distance, wanting, this wound,

no more.

On the Mukilteo Ferry, Returning

The mainland's wrapped in a blanket of rain, and we
are "in public," a coat three sizes too large. You cannot
be *with* me, we cannot say, *here, now,* only

this hollow of words like a stiffness, *hard weather,*
home. (The wind tears, the boat rips through it,

the pilothouse wipers flick like knives.) No
whisper of affection, no remorse. We feed the gulls
who flock behind us, mocking, a wither of crones.

(Like a bad knot things slip from the cleats, slide
through and we're free again, the heart

an empty hull, a bottle full of messages.)
How many lies — the ones that covered us, and the cold
comforts we return to, the lives in which we made

this space: a fire out of last year's pine,
then the wine, a decent Meursault. In that intense

and labile light, your skin an animal radiance,
I felt words resonate, yours and mine, giving them off
or hearing them. Fierce and tender, signing

whatever pain or sadness with the chest, or fucking
and laughing, cooking and eating. We have fallen

past something here, now, together, breathing.

The White Breast of the Dim Sea

A moon-snail burrows, buries his bone
in the rain-pocked sand, and this meek foot

extending, tender mucus-sheath.
A long labor.

Then I held you, still womb-wet, fumbling.
On the lip of the world,

the ship plows on, shudders, groans,
held close by the sea. Clouds spill

over the mountain like milk. Here are charms:
a half sand dollar, torn sand collar, blue hearts

and arrows, "Mother" on a sailor's arm.

Raccoon

Lies on the riverbank in a splash of wreckage,
driftwood, blue and green broken glass, rusted tin
on the dark sand, his matted fur wet and dull,
and the first flies, the whole body stiff
as from hard work, eyes open.

I'd seen him not a week before, handling
a small fruit or seed, plunging it in the river, eating.
You might have seen cleanliness, or the nerves
rising to the water's cold reveille, to better know
by feeling what he eats.

Watching his small, stocky frame amid the junk,
it was the work I loved, the hands gently
turning the fruit, then dipping, stroking, and
all the while watching the banks, reading
the air, the tips of his fur shining.

I feel his loss today, a grace
rough and sturdy, the minstrel face, the quick brush
of his tail bearing a ring for each year with the world.
All I can think to say to ease it

seems crude as the wreckage he lies in, that
he was at home with, is.

Transitions, Objects

For months the keys to your house sang in
my pocket, then that stone from La Push, a deep blood-
color on your tongue, figures failing

with habit into mass, volume, use. Snapshots,
stories fray from us, little strings
to follow into a deep wood. Sometimes your face

is picture perfect, as though someone, wanting
this bright artifact, had taken your soul
elsewhere. Don't move, you say, I'm

here. I remember things given away, the small
vitrine your daughter passed on to mine, and how
strange she found it cleaning

my daughter's room, to find the bric-a-brac new,
herself unable to take herself away.

Under the Bridge

Here between the stone fence and the meandering stream,
along the open lawn, through old groves of maple and white oak
richly crowned, a family spreads a last picnic of the season.
The house is of cut stones, large enough to persuade us
it has stood forever.

Behind us, the trampled grass, broken twigs, an occasional
distinctive print.

When I reach toward you it is as though I reached
from land's end, maybe, or beyond. A ravine in a city park,
a dark night, a bridge—the understructure
rotten enough that it is held
to foot traffic. A child

wanders in the spotless kitchen of a stone house.
(Time's wound, where she held him, never touching the water.)

*

But a father is something to travel for, hard-pressed. Today
we work on his car, a little radio-controlled all-terrain vehicle,
the new Lexan body spray-painted lime green. He has hand-painted
the roll cage black, but poorly, the lines fraying into the body
like neglected rope. He is a soft boy, and sweet, and I am irritated
by his sloppiness, his insistent childish what should I do now, how,
how, finding out the emptiness I would protect by making him
grow up too soon.

*

Under the bridge, some boys are playing on ropes swinging out
over the abyss to the other shore. What their faces show is not

pleasure but exhilaration tangent to terror as the pendulum
passes its perigee a hundred feet above
the sliver of stream.

At the Savannah

She wedges her two-year-old blond head
between the bars and will not budge,
waiting for all the slow grey bulk
implied by these muddy islands to rise.

They are content with things as they are,
these river hippos like broad peeled logs
pocked and gently lolling. Their valved
nostrils rise, and flare.

Out of the thick water, they move
as though prodded, great pads
of flesh shocked a little forward.

Nothing So Much As This

In the soft, full light of the rain forest, you gaze at the moss-hung
arms of the big-leaf maples, their great auburn shagginess an orangutang
stilled mid-gesture, and everywhere the air of something living always,
as in this colonnade of cedar, their buttressed roots rising
from the fallen nurse log

                 like a man from his body or a tomb.
Your heart is still, knowing they are near (because our joy was in
ourselves), around the corner (because our anger turned them in-
side out like a sweaty shirt), under the shadow of your hand:

                           her body
next to yours entering sleep as a cast on a child's arm breaks open,
and the tiny orgasmic twitch where she touches you, arms on your
chest, thigh against thigh,

                 and the rising heat of her mons tucked
against your ass. From the trees hang mosses with their leafy sex,
and from the mosses liverworts, thalloid and leafy, species
commingling life after life. This was your mission: L-100,
the date August 9, a covert running of guns and butter (because
our pain betrayed them

                 and our failures emptied them) for which
you believe you are a hero, commended by the Secretary of State
over late cocktails, for a "great job" over there, though
which job he didn't say, or where, and the actual mission postponed
on account of rain to August 11, on which evening a plane circled
half an hour

             above Honduran jungle. And each place you depart from,
lover's or friend's, you hear the doors on your heart opening
at 30,000 feet (because our sadness was a rebuke, a judgment, a
failure of nerve and gratitude):

                 the sound of air rushing past
(in a desert where there is too much water or none at all)
like a man coming back to the weathered house she asked him

to leave, knowing as he drives down the street, turns right
up the drive, careful of the big wheel, the skates,
a reflex
     and a feeling he has known and not known, a longing
that has been with him always for what he has lost,
and from which he feels severed,
                     still, or as the severed part, asking
what he did wrong, what turn he might have missed.

Into the Open Sea

Bodies are lovely in firelight, the lone bell
clanging at sea. Under the fire's breath,
your tongue
         on my nipples sends sea-
swell, current, doubling me like a swan.
Undressing, you were a shy girl scurrying
to hide your eyes
            so as not to be seen.
I had pictured your clothes falling like air,
your hands soft against your legs, and the
exquisite cranelike
          step from your panties,
your body golden and long. Your fingers
tighten on my arms.

A stone fisherman looks out to sea, and in
the marina an empty slip. They are corks
on water, there is
         shifting weather, work
any hour hauling from that alter world
a life to sell. The spirit fills us
or doesn't,
        and death's green sea has us
trying hard to get somewhere, though where
isn't for us to say.
A quiver
        enters my chest as you slip
your finger in my ear or suck it, draw it
wet across my lips or tongue.

The little pill of *freedom* dissolves
in bodies and signs, histories,
fear. Crossing the ditch
         of effort, need,

what pleasure comes, is taken in that fierce
forgetting, by turns passionate
and tender,

       taking everything it can.
I bite your cheek, then your breast or you
are lost in my skin, here streaming
into the open

       sea, your hair floating,
the jetty in floodlights at the river's
mouth, the open

       slip, weather massing
the largesse of the sea.

And a Small Cabin Build There

The light changes, and the sudden pedestrian surge
catches you, hands deep in your pockets,

reconstructing scenes: the young Swiss immigrant
sweating two jobs, English at night, Pinkertons,

for Sundays at Rye Beach, and still he's no American,
lost (where are your papers, then?) somewhere

in transit. All eyes are on you (they are going
about their business) corrosive as salt.

You carry what you love like a child. Set it down you'd be
helpless as a peeled tree.

And the man at long last pulls from his chest
the bad marriage, fearing he will bleed

from the wound opened in "husband," "lover."
No more than a man

who loves. Yet you'll have to leave it as
it is, good for something if not

good enough for you. Like a man in a suit
big enough for two, moving easily

in most directions, and in others constrained, maybe,
or unable to show effort, unable, maybe, to move

or talk. Who could know? Yet you were dry, always,
and barring little drafts, well-protected.

Out in the street now, you watch your step, sheltering
a retreat, the glade teeming with finch song, and walk

a little different from the rest just like you.

In the Community Garden, the International District

What you see from the street below is a steep
hillside, terraced and braced with railroad ties,
the individual plots segregated by various forms of wire
to which someone has tied strips of brightly colored cloth.
I should be happy, I think: nine months out

of that marriage I lived in like a child
in a greatcoat, I have grieved and felt my life
return. Content among friends, I have loved you without reserve,
wanted you more believing your arrangements wouldn't give.
And here you are tearing them up, scattering them like shells,

and I am a sullen, irritable child. On a bench at the top of the walk,
three street people are sharing a bottle in a paper bag. Some days
the emptiness announces itself like a birthmark or the inclination
to a bad habit. "Street people": as though they were asphalt,
or agglomerated stone. We wonder about the large head

that from a distance seems covered with broad green dreadlocks.
Close up we see the individual thick and crinkled leaves, and
recognize the plant as the one in the Jim Dine print where
it sits on top, labeled "K," above the turnip, "J," which
Dine's labeled "The World." Finally we agree it's kale.

The emptiness, a pool of it, nothing will fill it, as in the glass
paperweight my ex-wife gave me, cool and smooth and fitting perfectly
in the hand. Colors swirl through the clear glass, and in the center,
a black tear, nothing, until you look at it closely: a dense
cluster of green. The print is mostly hearts

like a child's potato prints — the color splotchy, washed out
here and there — and named after cities, restaurants, places the globe-

trotting lovers might have gone. The kale and root crops look real, and the turnip's stems and roots are cut as though for the table. Good food. (An old woman is filling her bucket with kale.)

At My Daughter's School

She has the rat nestled like a violin
between her shoulder and neck, and she's in-

troducing us, Rocker and Thumper, two doves and
a blazing fish. She lives

fully with this small handful shuttling
around her, settling

chattily to count pennies, nickels, dimes
on a meter stick. Time

washes over us. She reads
a story she's composed, the teacher's

written, underlining as she goes.

What Anyone Really Wanted

is hard to say, everything being so intense, only I couldn't
stay with any of them for long. Something was missing, always
the same piece, a mouth or the sun, and I'd see
in its absence the scuffed

linoleum and leave, as my mother had or those actual
women in movies at the end of the war, who would of course
quit work to raise their children, isn't it
what I always wanted?

Sometimes I'd be gone to cure cancer or make
a terrific priest. Sometimes I'd be gone a long time
when I finally stopped seeing them, and I'd have to
make myself really hard to do it.

My grandfather, too, loved women, and told me
he was too old to fuck, but his girlfriend wanted him anyway,
wanted him to lay his cock between her breasts,
and he told my mother

to send me back outside to fight like a man (I was
frightened, wanted home) and she did,
but she had tied my hands (sweet boy!), and I was everything
and a disappointment.

And it was him the announcer meant, saying, we are honored
to have in our studio audience tonight the distinguished
former president of the United States. But he wouldn't
stand, though he knew he could

pass for Truman if they didn't ask him to speak. Here's
what I remember best: my father's "I'll have to tell your mother"
when I asked for help, and Lenore Terzakos
with the terrific tits weeping

when they announced President Kennedy had been shot.
Later we watched as the motorcade drove past the Book Depository
and the infamous grassy knoll, the good god slumping
into flesh as the bullets hit him.

Some Days, Father

I came after you, all feathers, afraid I would
take crumbs as a meal. Take, eat, you'd say, trying
to give me what I asked, longing as it

swept you out to sea. I stood there with your scattered
gifts, listening for your return. Your words
stilled water, but I could see you only,

as I see in the eyes of my lover's son
that he hates me for taking his mother away, that
he would not lose that freedom.

Currents race like wind over hills, the blown head-
lines tacked to the trees, banners of rage
and desire. And the coarse-

grained faces blank, helpless as we are
some days denying it.

A Poem of the Seasons

The dogwood in early summer casts
sweet shade, and the white

false flowers
foiling the flowers shine

like first love. Then its berries
are pellets of self-consuming flame.

Sometimes we have needed
to get away, wanting everything, breaking

everything less. In winter you can see
each branch of the tree

splinter and curve. The cracks
travel the slate-

grey shell of the sky, mind and heart
lines everyone will read.

In the Hearts of
His Countrymen: L.B.J.

The lights are out as you descend. Flashlight,
nightgown in hand, into history's clown show:
real blood everywhere. You go down
in swamp and chronicle thinking yourself Le Loi,

the Trung sisters liberating jungle.
There is a light at the end of the hall, your boys
over a pin-riddled map. Once Nguyen the Patriot,
now He Who Enlightens. You will not be first

to lose a war or in anyone's heart. Bad air,
fever and chill inscribe themselves in blood
like armies or landlords or occupying tongues.

You'll feed the little nigra kids, everyone
love you best. Jobs all around, a great society.
(The greatest was the lawgiver Le Thanh Tong).

Everything at Once

So the moon is tonight, its milky witness
fingering the least apple petal, insinuating
a cool white hand into the ratchet of black-
berries. Its mottled eye thinks itself

a beneficent mother laving her child's eyes
as he stumbles, believing he can see more
than he can. Oh, alone, alone, who can

resist desire sliding down these lucid
assurances, a thicket of reasons
fat with fruit. The water has collected

in opalescent pools around the feet of old
statues. It is not safe in the park at night,
even though elections have been scheduled and
the army is with us, chatting and smoking.

A Gaze Blank and
Pitiless As the Sun

The air-raid sirens flail as you feather
your fifth carved arrow, "forever." You draw shades
against exploding glass, fall to your knees

and crawl under your desk, your head in your hands.
You see, risking your eyes, a delicate fringe

of lace, her scuffed shoes. You feel it in your heart:
she will wait for you. The city is in ruins, but a new
day dawns. Berlin has fallen. Moscow is ash.

Mallards dabble on the pond, and children are playing
nicely. A hi-fi plays "Soldier Boy"
and then "Candy Girl." A bottle spins its random

fifth-grade kiss. Over the desert, ten
thousand suns rise and set. So *My Weekly Reader,*
as a matter of technical information: this is a test.

Such Accomplishments

for Douglas Shields Dix

How the prospect draws us, the promise of an unrehearsed
satisfaction! We have moved from 0 and 1 to *maybe* or *this one
for now, this place,* always

less than we need, more than we can know. The pleasures of travel

are gone, nothing is toward or averting. I remember the final
copy sitting on my desk, a piece of me, certified, and how
inside me the darkness reared like a statue. Not

wanting what they want, you are the zero card, one foot
into what blackness. Yet you have climbed here, a white sun echoing
at your back the distant peaks, the snow, white rose

in your hand. Behind you a trace of movement across stone, deep prints
in the meadow. Listen, bird song chatters like a keyboard —

riddles of excess, a line of (f)(l)ight, and nothing between you
but the irreducible pleasure of the cry.

What You Told Yourself

Behind you, the clipped, plush grass is cool water lapping the trees. They stand in perfect rows along the winding promenades, or cluster in fruited groves, the air sweet and buzzing. Borne and taught here, playing with delight: this is your memory, though you have wondered, now and again, at the way it separates like a failed lamination, curling in.

A gate appears, and you see it as what you have been looking for without knowing it. Who could have detected that faintest whiff of irritation? After all, they gave you so much, this place, more than you deserve. And you have been happy, of course, though you could have been more grateful.

The gate presents itself, you must pass through it. Though the garden will be there, and no tangible thing stands between you and this past, you cannot return. Because it was not your past. Because the real fruit was plastic, and the sun a cheap fixture emitting a skewed spectrum of light. Sight has been what you told yourself, mixed in a jar where you threw the old paints.

Beyond the gate, a white landscape, brilliant by comparison, dazzling. That sack of instruments you have carried, accumulating more, will be useless here, you must put them down, though they have gotten you everything you have, accomplishments, praise, the stifling comforts of a predictable future that you can no longer choose, though there is a longing for that perfect fruit you can almost taste, the speckled light under the tall trees with the others where you belong.

Dark Eyes

The streets were wet, the gutters heaped with leaves. Smell it, you said, can you smell it, and I could feel you taking it in brisk currents of delight. Then sadness, a lengthening distance. As we drove home you said little, seemed farther. I thought about the movie, a life of luxury and excitement, the breezy, sexy, devil-may-care life of the bourgeois married into wealth, cute at forty, always half-*buffo,* the successful rake. In his sudden recognition that this life had left no trace in memory, I saw that I had forgotten all ethical questions in identifying with his quest.

I wanted you, was saddened by your distance, and was afraid to reach and be refused. I saw your appointment calendar open on your desk and felt jealous. I saw, meanly, the skin of your hands as you leaned over me, stroking my hair. Your breasts sweet hanging. I reached and kissed you, wanting you, and you came closer, your eyes saying you wanted me. We made love, then, sweetly at first and slow.

Two moments come back. There is his ease as he tells of riding into the Russian mist, crying he will return to the woman he loves, having crossed what bridges: and this is the end of his story. And I remember his face in that moment when the accumulated pain of his years of isolation at last displaces his garrulous, unflappable charm, like a death mask thrown off by a last, sudden breath.

After a Year, Some Words for You

Through the ravine between our houses or at the beach, reading
before the fire, nested like spoons.

They open to pain at a moment's deprivation, flooding the hour
with an age in the wilderness, confused by wind and sand.

How hard pleasure comes, guilt thrown in for a measure of good.

I've felt us fidgeting away. I saw you in dead earnest, hard, and far,
though the light was my longing.

And sometimes the pain collapses like a star, anger trapped with
the light, and I can see nothing else, not the light of others, not . . .

So that coming up the stairs to your house I am uncertain, for a moment,
that I have seen what I have seen, afraid that the house is dark,
tenantless.

We move into and out of each other's lives with tenderness and affection.

Talk bobbing, trolling, splaying its net.

The house afumble with children on the rope bridge of adolescence,
whispering will it hold, or this smaller one learning the world as a
sequence of hats randomized by desire.

(We is not, I is an other, and listening I know the heart is not one
but two, five, forty.)

So loving them, and so the long sweet moment after making love.

I feel you there, alike in what divides us, myself in your difference.

As You Stand Peeling an Orange

You are not beautiful in that way
that they have of becoming, albeit awkwardly now,
what they would make themselves seem;

nor in that way of the simple, the soft, the single
pure note held as time collapses in silence:
who might be anything, someday.

Then there is what my daughter sees as she
picks up, say, a stuffed bear, frazzled,
a little threadbare — something

that parted from her would be no longer
itself. Always *here,* always giving her herself,
what can it be but beautiful?

And finally, your favorite saying: at forty
we have the face we deserve. So it is
my daughter's face I see in my dream as I slap her

for biting me as we stand overlooking
Madrona Hill. A kind man behind her begins to sing,
having felt her face as I've seen it,

tumble back through evident shame to nothing,
begins to sing, rebuking me
and gently laying a path for her return.

At times I look with longing at my students' faces,
tablets bland in their way, blank,
that unfilled might fill this emptiness.

Such beauties are always elsewhere, really, and poor,
an accident of genes, the luck of the milkmaid's
pretty face. Yours are these and others:

what you have seen on your return, and the lights
you see by, this various radiance. As I write this,
I watch your feet, feeling drawn by their loveliness

too, watching you writing in your notebook, the pen
a steady shaking (that I must be so far
for desire, and the fear)

your left foot cocked left, digging in with your heel,
or the way you will stand peeling an orange,
your toes holding the ground.

The Banjo Lesson

1.

What is clear in the picture is their faces,
the rippling paint of the room sculpted stone,
their mutual gaze intense on the boy's right hand
plucking the strings. Tanner called it *The Banjo
Lesson,* the man seated mid-room, the boy standing
in the strong V of his thighs, willowy, knees bent
so that we know it is the man takes the child's weight,
the boy leaning hip and shoulder into the embrace

as into the buoyant water of a pool. My father
brought me there to learn to swim, the other kids
splayed across the water, on their backs, this one
spouting, a slight grimace at the chlorine's sharpness,
another's hands cycling at the wrist like wind-up toys.
A child too much alone, I could not believe that
the water would hold me, arms out, back arched.

The lifeguard taught me, his large calloused hand
in the small of my back, buoying me up, saying relax,
I'm here. He was a gentle man, easygoing unless
you pushed him, as kids would, and he let you know
he would stand where he said. His eyes as I see them
are sad, though I didn't see that then. I imagined
the chlorine had reddened them, although there was a
puffiness about them chlorine wouldn't explain.

2.

On the verge of living with a woman again, I know
I never saw a man live strongly in his own home, stand
lovingly for himself with the woman he loved. I find it

a cruel momentary irony that my ex-wife should have
taken a friend of mine and mentor as her lover, as
though I might have learned from him, who could only
repeat my subservience to her in spades. So sadly
busy chasing what ghost with his flurry of self-
improvements, he never saw this breaking of the bond
between us, this loss.

3.

Beyond the banjo's neck, a kitchen counter draped
with dishcloths, a dinner plate blanched by light. A
frying pan sits on the floor, one metal and one stoneware
pitcher at lower right. The student who is buying this

poster carries himself square-shouldered and stiffly, his
Lauren's, Calvin's, et al., composing around him an interior
of solitary mastery, an American original with books, manuals,
a few tools, seeing how he might make this accomplished, this

attractive a man. And although I cannot know it, I read in
his blank eyes that blackness I feel, a nihilism where
this black man and boy connect, and the necessary sentimental
representation that is an attempt to own what he has been

taught to deny himself, dependency, an open heart.

4.

Only that once do I remember my father finding a man
to teach me what he couldn't, and bitterly I would say
everything fell under that stamp. Though most often
alone, I have found mentors, a priest, a high-school

history teacher, a few therapists, good friends, and
learned, falteringly, to live in the quiver of feeling,
with some assurance, among men. Still the uncertainty
persists, and the longing, the undercurrent like
a stammer behind the achieved

compensations of performance, the public voice.

Teanaway River, Two Passes

1. Fortune Creek Pass

The stone hills draw along my gaze like a tide.

Five brown needles in a cluster, fallen on my shirt, and a grey furrowed bark, the tree slanting up over me, a little shade, and the needles in fat brushes at the ends of the branches.

How old these larches (600 years), how young the backcountry in which they grow. And to preserve this: always looking over our shoulders, bodies like threshers, and the dream of thought white on the mountains.

I imagine a hand tool drawn down the rock until it was clear nothing would come of it but talus and scree: the gouged face of a mountain beyond the pass, climbing. It opens the way the sky cannot, its uncertain distance expanding and contracting the frame like breath.

The wind, the clouds in time-lapse zooming by, and the intermittent rain. Each new line of hills adds two parts of white, receding into sky, the perfect picture, a precise sublimation.

That you sought me out for the same reasons as the others is only one way of talking about how we got here, not here, a barely perceptible stammer in a scene that lasts 10,000 years.

What connects is not pieces.

A stone like pale green glass, milky, and a cover of green grass, gentians, purple bells over the stream, a seam of it up the scrappy slope.

2. Long's Pass

Seeing no one but you for days, I am in and out of you like a
wind and the trees, the high wind on the pass, wheeling over the
edge.

Our tent is pitched by the river, and in the river is milk and
wine, and in the cooler fruit, cheese, veal.

If a tree falls, and another, a mown hillside with a road
scratched up it, what is it? We keep to the narrow trail to
minimize erosion, burn our toilet paper, bury our scat.

I hold back to see you, the ragged slopes where we collide, the
crust buckling under the strain, unable to give without giving
everything.

To look at a body with love, to touch it, rubbing a foot to open
the ache within the stiffness, each toe and then the ball of it,
running my thumbs along the high arch, each foot, watching your
eyes soften as the pain releases, full of affection.

In the mornings we bathe knee-deep in the stream, bending from
the hips and splashing, and in the afternoons lie in a shallow pool,
submerged, the brisk water shivering over us like fate.

What connects is not pieces.

When we make love, everything listens at the door, with us or
against us, and then leaves, so that when the door is opened,
there is this pass, a green valley at the foot of the mountains.

How I stretch you, you say, and how you lengthen me, and thicken.

Going down, it closes, decomposes itself again and again, composing this valley or that, this life. And always this desire wanting itself, or the desirer himself or herself, to be given over whole by the returning tide.

In Blue Lagoon

They march from the fallen leaves at the jungle's margin
on the sand, their skinny ochre legs
a sequence of diminishing stills neatly superimposed.
They bear the demeanor of snail, the whorled
body-well, stippled crimson, the color of moss, white
marble filigreed gold. Thus

armored, their errant path leads to the Straits

dim with algae bloom, bearing an ancient traffic
in charcoal, black sauce, salt eggs.
From the river's mouth, the massive barges, teak
beams bent laboriously by palm torch, hand-
hewn, drift upriver with their cargo and the tide.
(At the *Kastam* dock, a smuggler's boat,

pungent with clove; and Melaka's last English official,
the Custom Agent, Karim Abdullah Clark.) Six Chinese kids

are ambling down the stairs to the beach
where I have been watching sun-dazzle on the wind-scales,
the marching crab. *Hello* opens twice, three times
in their flutter of what dialect I couldn't say
as they jostle down past me laughing and shoving.

The youngest turns to me, still speaking, pointing
to the sea, perplexed and smiling.

A Poem for the Winter Solstice

I was coming down the stairs to the parking lot, and he was crossing my path at a right angle on the landing. I decided that I would give him money when he asked. He stopped and looked away as I approached, but a sound came from him — its intent was clear — and without looking I put a handful of change into his hand.

And I feel a little ridiculous saying this next thing, but I was stunned by the softness and warmth of his hand. If I had looked then I might have had to take him home, but I didn't think that then, I didn't look. I only took away the touch, his warmth, the cold around it.

In the story, Christ was born into poverty to accept the bruise of the Fall. It was God's choice for him.

Why this seems urgent now I don't know. Maybe it's a fear for the world my daughter will inherit,

that my place in the world is a margin, a sound without intent.

Or notice that warmth dies when the heart closes (because the pain was too much and there was nothing I could do about it):

so it will not do for me to say, to these friends only, or to equivocate between self-interest and greed, which not only believes in "the real world," fortuity, serendipity, but moralizes them.

(All our talk of "the needy," "the homeless," as though they left their shelters and emptied their stomachs this time of year to give us our charity.)

And the statistics, themselves little acts of cruelty: one child in five lives in poverty. In Seattle, three thousand two hundred people are homeless, there are thirteen hundred available beds—

amid the figures of excess, dissatisfaction always, and things made to fill it; and the economics of pain and privation on which it depends—

feeling a man's warmth, and the cold around it.

The Wax Sayadaw

is unnerving, a little too lifelike in the glass case beside
the president of the monastery association. They wear identical
saffron robes and black-framed glasses. Our Burmese hosts display

them with unself-conscious reverence, a quiet pleasure in
their good works that leads us rightly to the case of Buddhas.
They stand, sit, recline, their hands

variously positioned, though I cannot see that this is
"Indian style" or "Pagan, of course" or Sukhothai. Otherwise

the room is large, high-ceilinged, bare. The Buddhas are
mostly seated, the left hand face upward in the lap, the right down
across the right knee, fingertips to the ground (that

witnesses enlightenment). But this one, standing, its hands
at its sides, a clear shell encasing the gaily
colored organs: I know it, American style: the Visible Man.

The women of the house bring "tea" and "plain tea."
"You will notice that these Buddhas all share one hundred
and eight characteristics" specified by the *Digha Nikaya*

and that the plastic man is an amalgam of organs and
fluxes, dying. The patriarch of the clan enters and we stand.
He is ninety-four, "still has his mind, and will understand

English." We sit and chat. And when it is time to leave, the men —
our friend, his somewhat older cousin, and his uncle, fiftyish, still
looking under forty — kneel before him and with their arms

outstretched touch their foreheads to the ground, three times.
Outside, the boy is still guarding the car, and the rains have come,
warm and soft and furious.

The Straits of Malacca

The Muslim schoolkids plash in the Straits, going only
so far into the blue-crisp sea. It abounds with cuttlefish
and snapper, prawns and the ancient maleficent spirits.
The young women, evidently oppressed, splash in their plain
skirts and blouses, in radiant abandon. So

here we come, Americans in Mediterranean trunks, our matter-
of-factness and acute self-consciousness, the one tree
falling in the forest and we're always heard. We come bearing
natural beauty and physical culture, irresistible as the current
angled against the waves. (In the lone traveler only

do the sarong, the fez, and the five daily stations of prayer
take hold.) We drift south

regulating the salt content, the time of delay, the maximum
permissible height of the waves. Social relations remain
anyone's guess. Though the fishermen have warned you, no
women on the boat, no swearing or promises, no names and no
whistling, the spirits have you by the lips

saying *freedom, my freedom,* as though desire was not this
maelstrom surrounding your little boat. Be brave, we say, be
brave, this is nature, the sea is free of dark spirits, and sunset
the only object of your longing. There are new things to do, new
places to see. You will sleep in, awake to wonder

at the roaring chasm, *my body, my mind,* alone with them
on the crowded beach, thinking. And this is natural as anything,
the sole mortal thing you are, the necessary solitude
of your death having burrowed backward like a virus erasing
all connections and silences, all

but this terrific expanse of the sea, this freedom.

About the Author

Robert McNamara has experience in many manifestations of the published word. He was graduated from Amherst College (B.A. 1971), Colorado State University (M.A. 1975), and the University of Washington (Ph.D. 1985). While in Colorado he founded and was editor for L'Epervier Press, which is devoted to publishing contemporary American poetry; he worked as a printer, taught at Colorado State and the University of Colorado; in Seattle he wrote and published criticism on Pound and Eliot, kept L'Epervier afloat, and taught composition. He is now a lecturer in the English department's interdisciplinary writing program at the University of Washington. With an NEA creative writing fellowship in 1987–88, McNamara gained time to write this book. His poem "The Wound" received the *Kansas Quarterly*/Kansas Art Commission Poetry Award for 1987–88. His home is in Seattle.

About the Book

Second Messengers was typeset on the Compugraphic MCS 100 in Times Roman with Trump Medieval poem titles and part numbers in Schneidler Black Italic. The composition is by Lithocraft, Inc., of Grundy Center, Iowa. The design is by Kachergis Book Design of Pittsboro, North Carolina.

WESLEYAN UNIVERSITY PRESS, 1990